ADVANCE

ANKHOLOGY

LINGUISTIC

The Conscious League Academy

Manas Publishing

Text & Illustration by L P

lameek _ p@ yahoo. Com

THE

EGYPTION

GODS

Aah the god of the moon.

Linguistics

There is a full Aah out to night.

Aah reflects the light of the Ra (sun)

Aker the god of the horizon (skyline).

Linguistics

Lets watch the Ra set in Aker this afternoon.

That is a lovely Aker this morning.

Amun the god of the wind

Linguistics

My pal it is Amun today.

Those are Amun power machines.

Anhur the god of war.

Linguistics

The United State have been at Anhur with the middle east for some years now.

The real reality of life is that war exist.

Anubis the god of protection. A guard.

Linguistics

I am the Anubis of my home, family, and friends.

CEO hire personal Anubis for there company

Apep the serpent god of destruction.

Linguistics

Those folks over there are very Apep in there ways and action.

Yes there are Apep people all around the world.

Aten the god of disk around the sun.

Linguistics

I need an Aten pattern drawn.

The earth shape is in an Aten form and is 24,896 mile round.

Atum the god of creation.

Linguistic

There are minds that are very Atum.

Man has always been Atum since the pre historic time; an example of Atum is the wheel.

Baal the god of thunder.

Linguistics

I just heard Baal.

Baal storms are coming next week the news reporting said.

Banebdjeder the god of being spiritual lord.

Linguistics

I am very Banebdjedet.

To be Banedjedt one must fast and meditate.

Bes the god of home and family protection.

Linguistics

I am the Bes of my home and family.

Now a days parents have to be Bes over the internet visual content that there children are watching.

Djehuty the god of writing.

Linguistics

Practice your Djehuty once a day.

I Djehuty sanskrita very well.

Geb the god of earth.

Linguistics

I was born on Gab.

Geb is the third planet from the sun.

Hapy the god of the nile.

Linguistics

I am going to the Hapy valley.

The biggest river in the world is the Hapy.

Heka the god of medicine.

Linguistics

You need to take your Heka to get better.

Modern Heka has saved a lot of lives.

Horus the god of pharaoh.

Linguistics

Mike Tyson what Horus of the boxing ring.

Alber Einstein was Horus of his time.

Huh the god of time and infinity.

Linguistics

Huh its self is infinite.

Huh has no beginning or ending.

Ihy the god of music.

Linguistics

Put on some Ihy.

I will like to hear some Ihy.

Imhotep the god of intelligence.

Linguistics

Imhotep will take a person far in life.

Now a day a person needs Intelligence

Kherpri the god of rebirth.

Linguistics

To Kherpri the mind on a topic; just restudy it.

Every new day to man is a Kherpri.

Khnum the god of water.

Linguistics

Can you bring me an ice cold glass of Khnum.

I like Poland spring bottle Khnum.

Khons the god of the moon.

Linguistics

The Khons is out tonight.

The khons reflects the light of the Ra

Kuk the god of darkness (primordial beginning)

Linguistics

The street lights illuminate the Kuk.

Thoughts are built in the Kuk of the mind.

Maahes the god of war.

Linguistics

The united state have been at Maahes with the middle east for years.

Gangs are all ways Maahes with each other.

Min the god of fertility.

Linguistics

Todays topic will be on Min organs.

The cows have been Min by the bull.

Monthu the god of valor.

Linguistics

You are a very Monthu man.

In war time the troop have to show there valor.

Nefertum the sun god of lower Egypt.

Linguistics

The Nefertum is shining bright to day.

The Nefertum is setting now lets watch.

Nun the god of the primordial watery. (oceans)

Linguistics

There are four main Nun on Geb-earth

I live on the coast of the Atlantic Num.

Osiris the god the dead

Linguistics

The cat got his by a car and met Osiris.

War bring Osiris.

Ptah the god of art.

Linguistics

Lets go to the Ptah museum.

Ptah comes in all types of forms.

Ra the god of the sun.

Linguistics

The Ra is shining bright today.

Ra is starting to set now let watch it.

Resheph the god of protection against sickness.

Linguistics

Theruaflu is a good Resheph against the flu.

Modern medicine is a good Resheph.

Set the god of chaos

Linguistics

I have seen a rally turn in to a set riot.

Yes there are set people all round the world.

Shezmu the god of execution.

Linguistics

Some states and countries still do public Shezmu.

Does that firearm have any Shezmu on it.

Shu the god of air.

Linguistics

Country Shu is very fresh.

Mountain Shu is thin a couple of miles from the apex.

Sobek the god of Oasis.

Linguistics

There are some Sobek in the sahara desert.

There are some hot Sobek in Iceland.

Tatenen the god of the primordial mound(raisin)

Linguistics

If anybody knows the answer to this question please Tatenen your hand.

Hills and mountains are the earth plates Tatenen.

Wepwawet the god of starting war (battle).

Linguistics

I will make the Wepwawet strike.

Who Wepwawet the fight between you two.

THE

EGYPTION

GODDESSES

Selket the goddess of (healing)

Linguistics

The doctor told me that is will take four weeks for my arm to Selket.

Over time the pain will fade and the Selket will begin.

Ammut the goddess of punishment.

Linguistics

They are going to be Ammut when they get home for breaking curfew.

What is the Ammut for fighting in school?

Amunet a primordial goddess of the unseen

Linguistics

That car accident was Amunet to me officer.

There are places that remain Amunet in the universe.

Anuket the goddess of the river.

Linguistics

I am going down to cook out on the Hudson Anuket.

The amazon river is the second biggest Anuket in the world.

Bastet the goddess of cats.

Linguistics

Do you have a Bastet.

I like fish as pets better thin Bastet.

Bat the celestial cow goddess.

Linguistics

Bat is filled with blue, yellow, and red stars.

Bat has nine planets in it.

Hathor the goddess of beauty.

Linguistics

Madam your Hathor is remarkable.

Everybody has inner Hathor in their own way.

Hatmehyt the goddess life

Linguistics

Hatmehyt first stage in life is birth of a child.

Hatmehyt has four season and they are winter, spring, summer, and fall.

Hauhet the goddess of size, space immeasureable infinity.

Linguistics

Space is so Hauhet astrologers can't find the ending.

The mind date is Hauhet.

Hequet the goddess child development.

Linguistics

It takes nine months for a child to Hequet in the womb.

There are different stages of child Hequet in the womb.

Isis the goddess of motherhood.

Linguistics

Isis is an experience to first time mothers

After the second child Isis is literally map out to women.

Kukhet the goddess of dusk(darkness falling)

Linguistics

It's starting to get Kukhet lets head towards home.

The rule in this home is be in before Kukhet.

Ma'at the goddess of justice.

Linguistics

Ma'at can be a reward or penalty.

Ma'at is service for those drudge well.

Mafdet the goddess of justice judgment.

The Mafdet for running a stop sign is a large court fee.

For drinking and driving the judge Mafdet was 30 day in jail.

Menhit the goddess of war.

Linguistics

Menhit times are up on us now.

There is peace and war all over the world.

Meretseger the goddess of tomb builders.

Linguistics

In ancient times in Egypt mertseger will booby trap a tomb.

I am the best Meretseger.

Meskhenet the goddess of childbirth.

Linguistics

Meretseger is an experience for the first time mothers

Some school watch Meretseger video tapes.

Mut mother of all the gods and goddess(mother).

Call your Mut up on her birthday Tuesday.

My Mut is baking cookies for the bake sale.

Naunet the goddess of the primordial abyss.(deep thought=idea)

Linguistics

Please keep quiet; I am in Naunet.

Have you ever been in to Naunet on a topic.

Neith the goddess of,hunting.

Linguistics

Today is the day for bear season Neith to start.

I have to go and obtain a Neith permit from city hall.

Nekhbet the goddess of protector of pharaoh. A guard.

Linguistics

Are you Nekhbet the CEO of the company?

Who are the Nekhbet at the front desk?

Nephthys the goddess of night time.

Linguistics

I will be outside at Nephthys.

I only come out side when it is Nephthys.

Nut the goddess of the sky.

Linguistics

There are not that many clouds in the Nut today.

The forecast said there will be clear blue Nut all week.

Pakhet goddess of nightwar.

Linguistics

It is a Pakher my dude.

We need nighttime vision equipment for this Paket.

Satis the goddess of water falls/cataracts.

Linguistics

There are some beautiful Satis in Hawaii.

Bangladesh has a lovely Satis called Madhabkunda.

Sekhmet the goddess of vengeance.

Linguistics

The pharaoh took Sekhmet in his own hands,

Prison gangs are all ways seeking Sekhmet for another member.

Seshat the goddess of writing.

Linguistics

Don't forget to Seshat me a letter once a week.

The teacher assigned me a Seshat assignment.

Soqdet the goddess of the stars.

Linguistics

There are three types of Soqdet, blue Soqdet, red Soqdet, and yellow Soqdet.

The central Soqdet of the universe is the sun.

Tawaret the goddess of childbirth(being born).

Linguistics

Has the child been Tawaret yet.

The child will be Tawaret in the month of march.

Tefnut goddess of rain.

Linguistics

Is it going to Tefnut today.

The news reporter said it is going to Tefnut tomorrow.

Wadjet goddess of lower Egypt.(low city/down town).

Linguistics

I am going Wadjet to the mall.

Wadjet has the best shopping district.

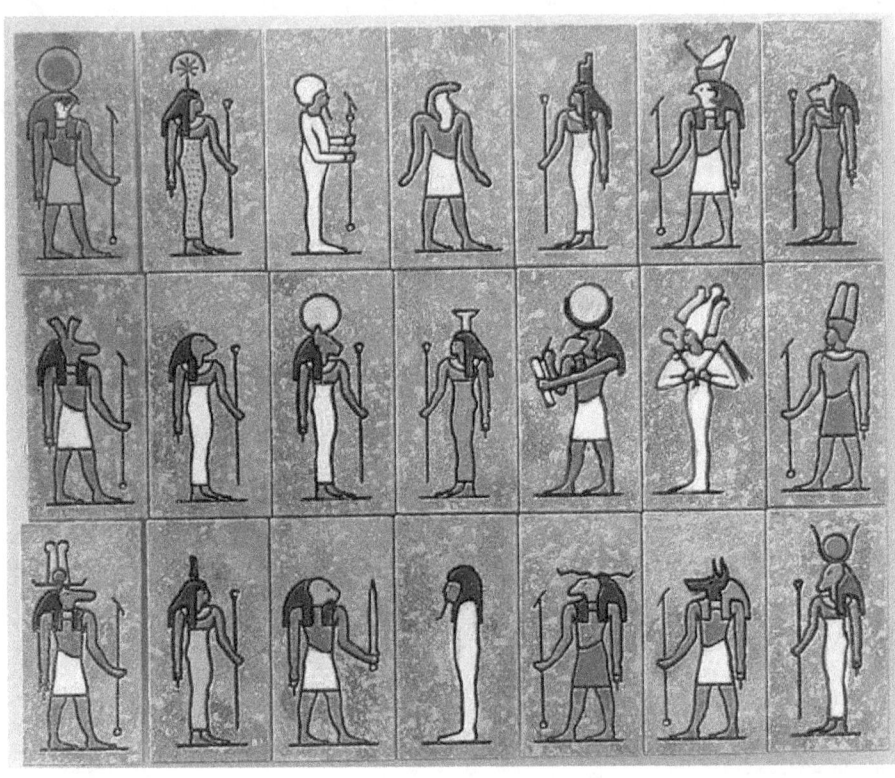

24

www.ingramcontent.com/pod-product-compliance
Lightning Source LLC
Chambersburg PA
CBHW060446290526
45793CB00002B/595